POCKET-SIZED PROSPERITY

Financial Shortcuts for Busy People

Alexander Kures

*To my many teachers, without whom
I would not be who I am today*

CONTENTS

CHAPTER 1: INTRODUCTION

The aspiration of many Americans is to live the American dream: a house, two kids, a 9-5 job, going on vacation, and celebrating a comfortable retirement. Most of the items that I just listed are only attainable when one's financial situation is secure. However, when it comes to balancing needs and desires with finances, people usually sacrifice their fiscal wellness at an alarming rate. If you don't believe me, consider these statistics from 2023:

- 68% of Americans say that their savings are not sufficient to cover their living expenses for just one month if they lost their job, and only 43% of Americans say they can cover an emergency of $1,000 or more with money from their savings.[1]
- 22% of Americans have no emergency savings whatsoever and 36% of Americans have more credit card debt than they do emergency savings.[2]

- 45.3 million borrowers have student loan debt, with an average balance of $37,388.[3] However, some studies suggest that 40% of borrowers **do not end up with a college degree**.[4]
- 55% of current workers plan to work in retirement, with 36% of these individuals citing "making ends meet" as the primary reason.[5]
- Individuals between the ages of 55 and 65 have, on average, $408,000 in their retirement savings. Simulations show that spending $75,000 per year would deplete this portfolio within about 13 years.[6]

As a nation, we are living well beyond our means, and the price we pay is living very stressed lives and having sub-par retirements to show for it. While money does not solve all problems, financial wellness is an important part of a balanced and fulfilling life. To promote the health and wellness of our communities and the country as a whole, we must take care of this aspect of our well-being.

This is a book I wanted to write to combine different opinions to get a bare-bones perspective on how to handle personal finance. I am not a financial advisor, and this is not meant to be an advanced guide by any means; rather, it is meant to serve as a core foundational piece of a rich financial life.

Let's get to the next chapter, which will solidify your purpose for the steps you are about to take toward fiscal responsibility.

CHAPTER 2: STEPS OF FINANCIAL WELLNESS

This short book will hopefully give you a lot of ideas on how to build a good life financially. The last thing I want to come from this book is a lot of disorganized tips and facts. Because of that, I wanted to provide the basic steps that I think are most important in paying off your debts and developing a healthy life. I've listed the steps below, and I will dive more into how to execute these steps in the next chapters. Be sure to complete each step in order, and don't move onto the next step until the previous step has been completed. Feel free to come back to this list as needed as you continue with this book.

1. Develop a plan for your financial journey.
2. Save up a $1,000-$3,000 emergency fund.
3. Pay your high-interest debt (above 4%) except

for your mortgage.

4. Build up your emergency fund to cover six months of expenses (not income).

5. Contribute to your 401k up to your employer match.

6. Simultaneously take care of the following, in accordance with your plan:

    1. Put 20–25% of your income towards retirement.

    2. Plan and save up for larger purchases.

    3. Make the minimum payments on your low-interest debt.

    4. Contribute to 529 plans for children.

    5. Pay off your low-interest debt.

7. Take time to enjoy the prosperous life you have built for yourself.

If you take **NOTHING ELSE AWAY FROM THIS BOOK**, please consider the information from these steps. If you simply follow the steps above, you will likely be in a better financial position than 90% of Americans within the next 5–10 years. This is the major lesson of the book, and reading ahead will continue to ingrain these values with strategies and practical examples. Let's get to it!

CHAPTER 3: DISCOVER YOUR DREAM

Here's a question that I hope you're asking yourself at this point: why should I care about personal finance? Ultimately, that comes down to you. Perhaps you want to retire early. Others may wish to ensure they are on track to meet their financial goals while simultaneously living an enriching and fulfilling life.

I believe life is too short to be unhappy. I dream of being in a life position where I work because I *want* to, not because I *have* to. I am planning on buying and owning a home on the West Coast and enjoying the natural beauty of the area with my family. I am making travel a priority, going to places like Cancun, Thailand, Europe, Vancouver BC, and the countless national parks in the US. I want to get the most out of life that I can, and the money I earn over the course of my career is an important tool to make my plans a reality. Because of this, I want to have a plan for where my money is going to meet those goals.

Many financially successful individuals say that the main ingredients to developing wealth are behavior and discipline. Generating an amount of money that lets you do whatever you want isn't hard if you follow some of the steps that have already been outlined. That's the easy part. The hard part is sticking with it, especially during difficult times. That is why this first step is so critical: it will give you the dedication to make it to your vision of the future.

Take some time for self-reflection to decide what your main motivations and vision for the future are. If you have others that are a part of your financial life, such as a spouse, sit down and discuss your vision with them. Here are a few questions that you could consider asking when developing your vision of a good life:

- Do you want to be married? What will that person be like?
- What sort of career do you want to have? How much time do you want to spend working in this career each day, week, or year?
- When you aren't working, what do you want to do? With whom?
- What are some items you are willing to splurge on? Why?

- What is your favorite activity or hobby? How could you do more of it?
- When do you want to retire?
- What does retirement look like for you?
- Do you want to leave an inheritance after you are gone?
- When you look back on your life, what do you think your happiest moments will be?

Make sure you go through these questions and other aspects that are important to your particular life scenario as well. If you do this, I promise that it will be easier to develop a solid financial plan and stick to it. Sometimes you have to know where you're going before you start the journey.

CHAPTER 4: BUDGETING

There is a saying that proponents of a budget use that goes something like this: a budget will allow you to tell money where to go, as opposed to wondering where it went. It reveals a significant amount of information about your spending habits and saving patterns, and even allows you to develop a plan for future purchases or debt payments. Budgeting is one of the most technical parts of a healthy financial life; therefore, understanding how to use it is critical.

Budgeting Platforms

There are a number of mobile apps that can be used to easily budget for you, such as EveryDollar, Simplifi, and PocketGuard. Some of these have free versions, but many budgeting apps require you to pay for them. My wife and I use a document on Google Sheets that you can find in the appendix (along with a guide on how to use it). Whatever you end up using, the basic premise is simple: each dollar that you earn should be accounted for in your budget. What goes in as income goes out as expenses, savings, or investments.

How to Use a Budget

There is one basic tenet when it comes to budgeting, and that is that money in equals money out. You don't want to finish the month with money left over or having spent too much money; you instead want every dollar to be accounted for.

It's important to sit down at the beginning of the month and make a plan. How much do you expect to spend on groceries? How about gas for your car? Is there a birthday this month that you must account for? The total amount you expect to spend in a month should not exceed what you expect to earn.

At the end of the month, it's important to sit down and go over your budget again. Were there areas where you spent more than you meant to? How about areas where you didn't spend as much as you would expect? Understanding these trends gives an important glimpse into your behavior and helps you set more realistic spending goals for the future.

If this is your first time budgeting, I suggest taking the first 2–3 months to simply track your spending. Try to predict how much you will spend in each category, and then see how you did at the end of each month. It's amazing to see how quickly certain costs add up to high amounts. Therefore, give yourself a grace period to act as a "reality check" to help you inform a more realistic version of what your budget should look like for the future.

How Much to Put in Each Category

How you break down your budget is fairly important as well. Overspending or underspending in different areas can tip your life out of balance. The key to maintaining a successful budget is to be realistic. It's much easier to maintain a budget when you allow yourself room to realistically live your life. The main categories of your budget will be debt, rent/mortgage, living expenses, savings, investing, and "fun money." The descriptions of these categories are as follows:

Debt: The amount that you send out to pay your combined loans, with the goal of paying them off (not just meeting the minimum payment).

Rent/Mortgage: The amount that you spend on housing to put the roof over your head.

Living Expenses: Any living expense that you pay that is not considered under Rent/Mortgage. These include things like groceries, transportation, utilities, internet, pet food, and others.

Savings: This is how much you contribute per month to keep your emergency fund in a good place, as well as things like planning trips or preparing for large purchases that don't normally fit into the budget.

Investing: How much you send to your 401k, Roth IRA, and other taxable accounts.

"Fun Money": Money that you have to spend on hobbies, shopping, nights out, and enriching your life.

The relative breakdown of each will change depending on which stage of life you are in, the balance of your debt compared to investments and savings, and so forth. Here are my suggested proportions for where your monthly paycheck should go.

	Debt with 6+% Interest	No Debt, >25 years old	No Debt, 25-45 years old	No Debt, 45-65 years old
Debt	40%	0%	0%	0%
Rent/Mortgage	20%	25%	25%	25%
Living Expenses	30%	30%	30%	30%
Savings	2%	5%	5%	10%
Investing	5%	30%	20%	15%
"Fun Money"	3%	10%	20%	20%

For example, if a family makes $100,000 per year and has $250,000 of total debt, I would suggest spending $20,000 on rent/mortgage, $30,000 on living expenses, and $3,000 on fun activities, hobbies, and travel. $5,000 would be invested in retirement accounts or the stock market, $2,000 would go towards padding your savings account, and the remaining $40,000 would be used to aggressively pay off the debt that you have.

An interactive calculator to work your income into this table will be found in the appendix.

The numbers that I have provided in this chart aren't rock-solid numbers; you can change them if you really need to. Ultimately, your financial plan is up to you. In fact, I strongly support having a monthly budget meeting, either on your own (if you're single) or with your spouse, to determine what is best for your particular situation. The first few meetings will be the most difficult. The initial 3–4 months may be frustrating as you compare how much you *think* you will spend in a particular area to how much you *actually end up spending*. Just remember that if you increase spending in one category, you must decrease spending in others to compensate.

The last thing I want to emphasize here is that a budget will only work for you as long as you use it. My wife and I were meticulous about saving receipts and logging our purchases into our budget the same day. The dedication and diligence we had allowed the budget to work for us. This is where your "why" comes in: keep your dedication, and your budget will truly be a valuable tool to help you take control of your spending habits.

That's a lot of detail, so feel free to go back and make sure you understand what all of this means. I wanted to summarize these ideas to help make them concise. When you are ready, proceed to the next chapter.

Summary

1. A budget is a summary of your income compared to your expenses. It should give you the ability to plan for the month, or even the year, and allow you to assign a purpose to each dollar you earn.

2. Your budget should be broken down into a few main categories, which show you how much you should spend on any given area at a time.

3. Have a monthly meeting, either on your own or with your spouse, to discuss how what you actually spent contrasts with what you *thought* you would spend and adjust your future months accordingly. These meetings will take an hour or two initially, but will eventually take 5–10 minutes once you get the hang of it.

4. To make a budget work, you must be dedicated, diligent, and realistic. If you are not, it is impossible to make the budget work for you.

CHAPTER 5: DEBT AND MONEY MISTAKES

Americans have been sold the idea that we must be consumers. If other people have something, we deserve to have it too. This has led to an inability to plan for large purchases or subscriptions, especially because we make way too many. Debtors take advantage of something called compound interest, which is when your future interest accumulation is determined by the original amount you take out plus any interest that has already accumulated. This allows the debt to grow to astronomical proportions.

It is true that certain low-interest loans can be beneficial, allowing you to increase your earning potential and set yourself up for a better situation financially. In this sense, small debt can be paid off over time so that money can be invested to outearn whatever interest would accumulate. In the suggested steps of financial wellness, I suggest only racing to pay down debt that has an interest rate of 4% or greater. Larger interest debt will continue to grow until it is insurmountable, so this needs to be gone as soon as possible.

Live Simply

At this point, I must warn you. If you have a high debt burden, paying it all off is going to be difficult. This is where your conviction is going to be tested the most. In my suggested budget, I allow a meager "fun money" allocation of 3%. This should be just enough to allow you to enjoy life while almost half of your income is sent towards paying off debt.

There are two ways to find more money to contribute to debt: either work/earn more, or spend less. It's important to sit down and take a hard look at what you have and what you can do. A few steps to consider:

- Cut down to one streaming service, or even better, cut them out entirely.
- Have a yard sale and get rid of clothes, toys, or tools that you don't use.
- Cancel your gym service. Go on runs, work out in a park, or use a cheap gym instead of the nice designer yoga studio with the fancy water.
- Pick up extra shifts at work or take advantage of overtime opportunities.

> Consider getting a part-time job or starting a side gig.

- Meal plan and cook at home instead of going out to restaurants.
- Consider selling your expensive car and buying a used vehicle with the cash from the sale to get rid of your monthly payment.
- Get rid of your expensive toys. Boats, RV's, ATV's, and the like all need to go. Now.
- No more vacations until debt is paid off.

This list isn't exhaustive, and you can find other ways to get more money to crack down on your debt! The point is that you want to find a way to send as much money as you can towards beating down high-interest loans and getting out of the hole you're in. If you make these difficult choices now, I promise that the future will be so much more fun and bright.

Understanding your Debt Repayment

Before we talk more about paying off loans, there are a few basic terms you should be familiar with. Your principal is the original amount you borrowed for a loan. The interest rate is essentially the "fee" that you must pay for taking out the loan. Interest will continue to accumulate on whatever unpaid money you have taken out. Therefore, debt is the total amount that you owe on a loan (the principal plus the interest). A minimum payment is a dollar amount, usually agreed upon when you take out the loan, that you must pay every month to avoid late fees and penalties.

Now that you better understand how your debt works, let's quickly go over a few ways to pay off your debt:

- **Send more money.** Essentially, work overtime or sell your property to help generate money to pay off your debt. What may be even better is to sell items that are keeping you in debt. For example, sell the new car that you own to get rid of your $500 monthly payment. This will clear one source of debt and free up a significant portion of your budget.
- **Negotiate**. You can ask to have your interest rate lowered or even temporarily paused. You can also request that 20% of the loan be forgiven if you pay off the other 80% on time. Keep in mind, though, that the best leverage that you have as a negotiator is showing yourself to be reliable. Be sure to pay all your loans on time, no exceptions.
- **Debt Snowball vs. Debt Avalanche.** There are two schools of thought on how to pay off debt, which I will use an example to explain. Let's say you have the following debts:

For both the avalanche and the snowball methods, you must pay the minimum monthly payment on the debt that you have. Let's make an example of some debts to pay, shown below:

	Principal	Interest Rate	Minimum Monthly Payment
Auto Loan	$ 15,000.00	4.50%	$ 450.00
Medical Bill	$ 2,500.00	2.40%	$ 75.00
Credit Card	$ 3,000.00	25%	$ 150.00
Student Loans	$ 2,500.00	7.00%	$ 375.00

For this example, your minimum monthly payments add up to $1050 per month. The **Debt Snowball** works by putting as much extra money you can into the debt with the *lowest principal* (which is the initial amount you owe on the loan). If you rearrange these debts, here they are in order of lowest to highest minimum monthly payment:

	Principal	Interest Rate	Minimum Monthly Payment
Student Loans	$ 2,500.00	7.0%	$ 375.00
Medical Bill	$ 2,500.00	2.4%	$ 75.00
Credit Card	$ 3,000.00	25.0%	$ 150.00
Auto Loan	$ 15,000.00	4.5%	$ 450.00

You will make each minimum payment and pay an extra $200 per month towards your debt with the smallest principal. In this case, it is your student loans, meaning you will pay a total of $575 per month. Once you pay off the smallest debt, you take the full amount that you were paying towards that debt and apply it to the next largest debt. This means taking the $575 you were paying towards student loans and putting it towards the medical bill. This will allow you to pay $650 on the medical bill until it's wiped out, at which point that will be moved to the credit card bill. Continue this cycle, "snowballing" your total payments down the list until your debt is completely paid off (woohoo)!

The **Debt Avalanche** works in a similar way to the debt snowball, except for a small twist: you tackle the debt from the *largest interest rate to the smallest*. Take a look to see how that impacts the order in which we pay off our debts:

	Principal	Interest Rate	Minimum Monthly Payment
Credit Card	$ 3,000.00	25.0%	$ 150.00
Student Loans	$ 2,500.00	7.0%	$ 375.00
Auto Loan	$ 15,000.00	4.5%	$ 450.00
Medical Bill	$ 2,500.00	2.4%	$ 75.00

For this example, make all your minimum payments and put your extra $200 on the credit card. Once that is paid off, take that full amount ($350) and apply it to the student loans (for a total of $725) until that debt is paid off. Continue moving down the list this way until your debt is cleared!

Both of these strategies work, but there's a debate as to which one works better. Advocates of the debt avalanche will argue that your debt doesn't have as much ability to accumulate. Therefore, mathematically speaking, you will pay off your debt faster and with less interest accumulation using the debt avalanche. However, studies have shown that households are more likely to stick with debt repayment and be successful if they use the debt snowball method. This is theorized to be a result of having "small victories" early on, which provide motivation to tackle the larger debts. Take time to reflect and decide what debt payoff strategy is best for you. Then go out and get rid of that debt!

Protect Yourself While you Pay Off Debt

To prepare yourself to pay off debt, it is important to save up an **Emergency Fund**. This is a certain amount (many sources suggest somewhere between $1000-$3000) that you keep in the bank to use for *emergencies.* The only thing that this fund is used for are *absolutely necessary expenses* that would otherwise force you to take out another loan, such as auto repairs or medical emergencies. If you have to spend down your emergency fund, continue your minimum payments on your debt and build your emergency fund back up before continuing on with your debt payoff journey.

Avoiding Money Mistakes

I would be remiss if I did not discuss the common ways that people get into debt. Here are a few examples and how to avoid them:

- **Credit Cards**. Full Disclaimer: My wife and I own credit cards. We use them for a lot of our purchases and enjoy the benefits that come with them. That being said, credit cards **MUST** be used responsibly due to atrocious interest rates (up to 26%) and the ability to keep buying things even if you don't have the money. The easiest way to use them responsibly is to link them to your bank account and set up autopay to balance in full every month. If you don't have this level of self-control, get rid of your cards.

- **Being House Poor**. While home ownership is a part of the "American Dream," many people use this dream to justify the purchase of a house that is way out of their budget. Being house poor is when your rent or mortgage, utilities, and maintenance costs suck up so much of your income that you don't have money left over to live the life you want. To prevent making a huge mistake, here are a few rules of thumb to consider when looking to buy a house:
  - Be sure you include a 20% down payment when purchasing a house.
  - Seriously consider downsizing if you realize you're house poor.
  - Keep your house for 7–10 years to give yourself a high probability of breaking even when you eventually sell it.
  - Your house should cost no more than 2x your yearly salary. Another way

to look at it is that your payment should be no more than 25% of your monthly salary.

- o Rent for 1-2 years in the area before you buy property. This will give you a good idea of whether or not you like the area and prevent you from being forced to stay in an area you don't like.
- o If you cannot afford to purchase a home, there is ABSOLUTELY NO PROBLEM WITH RENTING.
- o A shorter term on your mortgage payment (e.g., 15 years vs. 30 years) will mean a higher payment up front, but in the long run you pay considerably less in interest.
- o As interest rates fluctuate, don't be afraid to look to refinance your mortgage to a lower rate.

- **Being Under-Insured**. Financial experts agree that you must protect against events that represent a significant threat to your financial situation. Medical emergencies, severe damage to your home, and disability are all examples of financial catastrophes that fall into this category. Be careful of *over*-insuring, as this will take more money than is worth your time. For example, while insurance for your phone breaking is helpful, replacing a cell phone is not a financial catastrophe and can be paid for with savings.

- **Auto Loans and Leases**. It's incredibly important to have a working vehicle to get you to your job and keep your family safe on the road. However, many people fall into the trap of buying an expensive vehicle they don't need. Even worse is leasing, where you pay for years only to not end up owning anything at the end of it. Buying a good used car can be a much cheaper alternative. You can also follow the Money Guy 20/3/8 rule, which provides a smart way to finance a new vehicle. This rule states that you make a 20% down payment and pay off the car in 3 years or less with a payment that doesn't make up more than 8% of your income.[7] If it isn't your primary vehicle, or if it is a luxury vehicle (not for everyday commuting), pay it off with cash. I understand cars can be fun and flashy, but don't let them drag you down into debt.

Debt is the biggest obstacle to your financial wellness. Clearing out debt as fast as possible digs you out of such a big hole, allowing you to hold on to as much of your money as possible. Ultimately, it gives you the opportunity to start building wealth and fulfilling your financial plan. After your emergency fund is in place, tackling your loans and debt is priority #1.

CHAPTER 6:
BUILD SAVINGS

A critical component of avoiding debt is having money available for immediate use. While you don't want to have all of your net worth contained in savings, a healthy savings balance is a vital component of getting rid of debt and living a healthy financial life.

The Importance of Liquidity

"Liquidity" is a term that is used to describe how quickly an asset can be converted into cash. For example, a house can be an amazing asset for you and your family. However, if you need that asset turned into cash, there is a good chance that will take quite a while, even years, to occur. That money is fairly illiquid, meaning it isn't easily converted to cash. Let's go over a few reasons why having liquid money is a good idea.

- **Emergency Fund**. As stated in the previous chapter, an emergency fund is your hedge against debt and financial ruin. Once your debt is paid off, your next priority is to build up your emergency fund so it covers about six months of living expenses. In the event you can't work, you will have a cash reserve to fall back on while you figure out a new plan.

- **Savings Goals**. This is where saving starts to really get exciting. You get to start saving for big-ticket items that are fun, like a vacation or an expensive toy. Better yet, save an extra 15% or so to cover any unexpected costs. Make a detailed, itemized list of costs, and begin saving with purpose!

- **Saving for Opportunity.** As you get more advanced in your personal financial knowledge, you will see that many people like to keep a "cash reserve" for opportunities that come their way. Having money on hand gives you the freedom to pull the trigger on short-lived opportunities that have a short window to act. When the opportunity comes, make sure you are prepared to take advantage.

Where do I Put My Money?

- **Physical Cash**. While it is extremely liquid, it is perhaps the worst place to store your money. It will not gain value with interest and is also very unprotected and exposed.

Therefore, an EXTREMELY small amount should be kept in cash. My wife and I probably have about $200 in cash at any given moment. In today's society, physical cash is not a powerful asset, so it isn't as needed as it once was.

- o Keep minimal assets in cash (gifts for nieces and nephews, money for gas or groceries, etc.).
- **Bank or Credit Union**. Banks and credit unions are good for protecting your money. It can grow with meager interest rates and is easily accessible via an ATM or a debit card. Setting up a direct deposit can ensure your paycheck goes straight to this account. Make sure that the bank is insured by the FDIC, which is the government's promise to reimburse you up to $250,000 should the bank fail.
  - o Keep 50% of your emergency fund in banks and/or credit unions.
- **High Yield Savings Account (HYSA)**. These are similar to what banks and credit unions can provide. Your money is a little less liquid than at a credit union, but they offer higher interest rates. At the time of this writing, the high-yield savings account my wife and I use has an interest rate of 4.8%, which is double the highest interest rate my credit union provides. Be sure to read about them

and make sure you trust them before giving them a substantial portion of your savings.

- Keep 50% of your emergency fund in HYSA's, as well as savings for items to be purchased within 3-5 years.

Savings are an important part of your financial wellness and open up a wide range of opportunities that are not present when you have no savings and high debt. The biggest danger of keeping your money in savings is that your money isn't allowed to work for you and generate more money. In the next chapter, we'll take a look at what to do with the money outside of your immediate savings.

CHAPTER 7: INVESTING AND RETIREMENT CONTRIBUTIONS

There are lots of get-rich-quick schemes or stories out there that show you the path to "quick" wealth. The problem with these is that they are often rife with scammers, failure, and false promises. The only way to reliably build wealth is to do it consistently over the course of your career. This is why it is important to live below your means. It gives you the freedom to save, live a good life, and put a significant portion of your money away to grow without lifting a finger.

I won't lie to you; this is the longest and most difficult chapter in this book. It's here because this is the step that is most critical to understand in personal finance. I tried to provide lessons and rationale to help you better understand what you are doing. You can do everything else in this book correctly, but if you don't invest or save for retirement properly, it can prevent you from building wealth. If done properly, this is the most exciting part of personal finance that will truly take your net worth to the next level.

Compound Interest is Your New Best Friend

Just as your debt can compound upon itself, so can your investments. Consider this basic example: There is an investment that consistently returns 20% per year. If you invest $100, at the end of the year, you'll have $120. During the next year, your money grows even more, reaching $144. The year after that, it's over $172. Assuming a constant rate of return, the total value of that asset will become greater and greater. When you do this consistently, the numbers add up at an astronomical rate.

Let's apply some more realistic numbers to this example. Let's say you contribute $200 per month to your retirement funds, for a total of $2,400 per year. If you contribute this amount for 30 years with no interest, you will have accumulated $72,000—no small number by any means! A graph of this growth will appear as it does below:

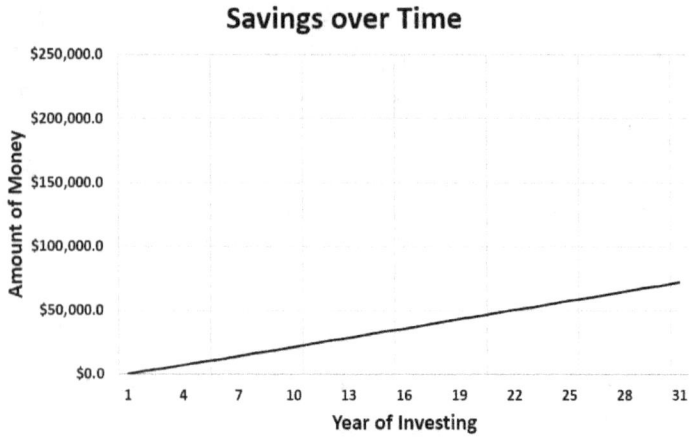

Now we will use the same numbers: $2,400 per year for 30 years. But instead, we will use a 7% compounding return, which is a widely accepted average return for the US stock market. The change this makes is astounding: You will end up with over $242,750! Think about it: that is more than 3x the amount that you originally put in! This is your money working for you.

Making smart, early investments changes you from someone with a positive net worth to someone who will generate wealth over their lifetime.

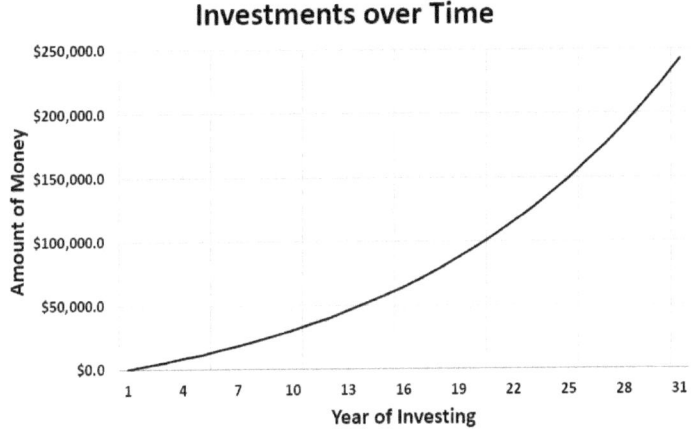

The 20% Rule

The total balance of your retirement portfolio when you decide to leave the workforce will largely depend on how much money you put into those accounts over the course of your career. One study showed that a retirement portfolio that is 25x as large as your current spending will maintain your current lifestyle throughout your retirement. In other words, if you spend $100,000 per year, you can reasonably expect to maintain your lifestyle if your retirement portfolio has at least $2.5 million. Another study by William Bengen in 1994 showed a similar finding: withdrawing 4% of your retirement portfolio each year would allow your portfolio to last for 30 years (essentially a full retirement from age 65–95) in almost any economic scenario.[8]

To get to this amount, most financial experts

state you should invest somewhere between 15% and 25% of your yearly income in retirement. The earlier you start your retirement contributions, the lower that number can be. This provides you with the flexibility to spend a significant portion of your income while also being able to prepare for the future.

Time in the Market is Better than *Timing* the Market

Stacy the plumber started a career not long after high school, and her average income over her career was $75,000. She started by putting 15% of her money away for retirement ($11,250 per year) and worked from age 20 to 65 for a total of 45 years. Her investments grew at an average rate of 7% per year.

John is also a plumber, but he didn't realize the importance of investing. He ends up out-earning Stacy by earning $100,000 per year. He decides to be more aggressive than Stacy's strategy, putting away 18% per year ($18,000), and ends up investing from 35 to 65 for a total of 30 years. His investments also grew at a rate of 7% per year.

Stacy earned $3,375,000 in her 45-year career and, as you can see in the graph, has a very nice $3,439,700. retirement account to fall back on when she decides to call it quits. According to the 4% rule, this will allow her to spend a whopping $137,588 per year in retirement! Way to go, Stacy!

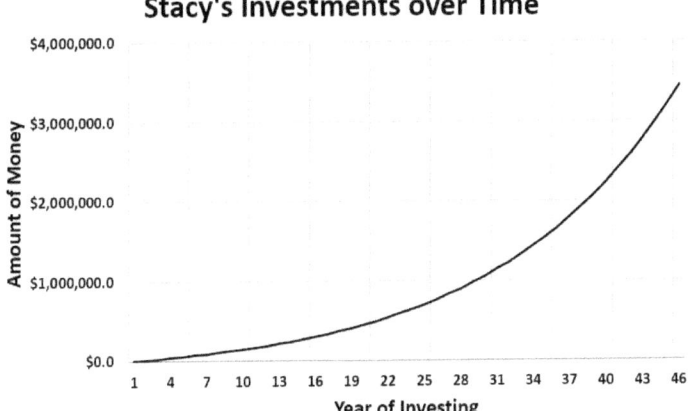

John earned a staggering $4,500,000 in his 45-year career. However, because his money had less time to compound, his retirement portfolio is much smaller, with a total of $1,819,314.74. This is despite the fact that John out-earned Stacy by over $1 million, and actually put $33,750 *more* than Stacy did in her retirement portfolio!

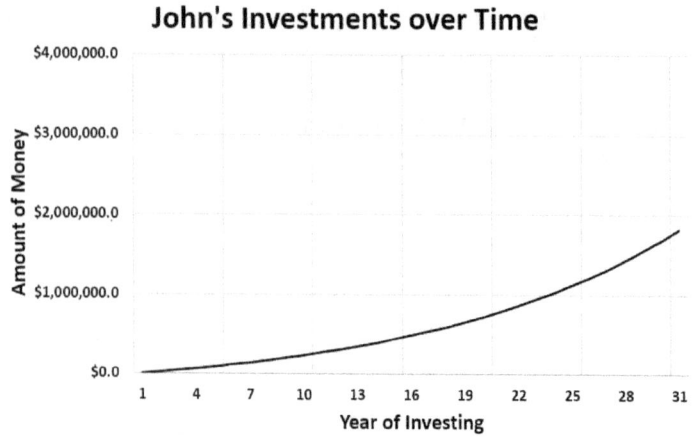

There is a very important lesson here: the longer your money is working for you in the form of an investment, the more room it has for potential growth.

PS: If John had invested the same amount he did for his whole career, like Stacy did, his retirement portfolio would be over $5.5 MILLION dollars!

Be the Market

One of the most common benchmarks that is used to determine a "winning" investment portfolio is the Standard and Poor's 500 Index, or the S&P 500. It was developed in 1957 by two merged financial data publications, the Standard Statistics Bureau and Henry Varnum Poor's publication on the financial operations of US railroad companies. Today, it is a measure of the 500 largest companies in the US that trade on the stock market and a general indicator of overall market wellness. Many people will brag about being able to "beat" the market, and what they usually mean is that the returns from their investments were greater than the proportional returns of the S&P 500.

So how often do people beat the market? It turns out, not very often. I will discuss more about what a mutual fund is in the next section, but it is pertinent to answering this question. As of mid-2023, somewhere around 10% of actively managed mutual funds (meaning an investor is managing the purchase and sale of stocks) have either met or beat the S&P 500 when covering a 15-year investing period. Many of these funds had a stretch of 1-2 good years and couldn't consistently outperform the S&P 500.[9] In fact, when looking at the top quarter of mutual funds in terms of performance, not a single one could maintain that top quarter performance for even a full calendar year.[10]

Keep in mind that these aren't your average water-cooler investors. These are highly skilled, highly technical, and professional investment experts. They have the ability to get news fast, run intense analysis on thousands of data points, and execute purchases and sales in fractions of a second. If *they* can't reliably beat the market, what makes you think *you* can?

Therefore, your goal should be a little lower

but still highly effective. Instead of trying to *beat* the market, work your best to *be* the market. The S&P 500 can vary widely from year to year, but on average, it has grown between 7% and 11% per year. Matching this average rate of return will allow your money to grow and for compound interest to take effect. Therefore, your goal year-to-year should be to model the growth of the S&P 500.

What Should I Invest In?

Investing your money can be a daunting task, with much confusion about how to analyze companies or specific groups. Many people make the mistake of buying a stock to turn around and sell it later. Most people do this because they have a feeling their stocks will go up. This is a strategy more akin to gambling at a slot machine than investing. When you invest, you purchase something because you believe in the intrinsic value of that property and its ability to grow. Therefore, don't buy something to sell it later. Buy something and hold it, and let that investment do the work for you.

What are the classic forms of investments that people use in their retirement or trading accounts? First up are **stocks**, which are fractional shares of a company or corporation. There are almost 7.5 billion shares of Microsoft available as of 2023, meaning that when you buy one share of MSFT (the stock symbol for Microsoft), you are now a partial owner of the company.

Stock prices change based on two things: the actual performance and value of the company (how it does), as well as the public sentiment of the company (how much people feel it should be worth). Looking day-to-day at stock prices, there is a high amount of volatility. However, with a longer investment horizon (years), the volatility tends to decrease. This is because public sentiment does not ultimately affect the actions of the company, and eventually profit and expansion speak for themselves. So don't judge the performance of a stock based on short-term performance; instead, evaluate how it does over the long term.

While stocks are extremely useful, **bonds** are often considered to be a much more conservative investment. You can think of a bond as a loan that you provide to an organization. This comes with a particular interest rate, which is paid at a specific rate (usually annually). Once the term expires (or the bond has reached the agreed-upon length of time), the company or government promises to pay you the full amount you loaned them. For example, if you buy a $1,000 5-year bond at 2%, the people who issued the bond will take your $1,000 to help their company grow. They will pay you 2% of that $1,000 every year ($20 per year) until 5 years are up, at which point they will return your $1,000.

Bonds have specific benefits and drawbacks. They provide a guaranteed positive return, despite whatever the rest of the market is doing. Therefore, you can use it to protect yourself against potential downturns in the stock market. The bad news is that if the stock market is doing really well and earning high returns, your money is locked away in this investment that is returning you a much smaller amount. The final drawback to bonds is that they are only as reliable as the entity that issues them. In other words, if a company you bought a bond from goes bankrupt and cannot pay you your bond back, you're out of money. So you must take the reputation of the organization issuing the bond into account.

When it comes to investing in stocks and bonds, it can be extremely difficult to know where to start. In fact, many people have squandered their life savings by putting their money into unwise investments. It is therefore important to **diversify**, which means you vary your investments over multiple vehicles (e.g., stocks and bonds) and industries. One investment failing would be bad, but your portfolio as a whole would not fail.

My grandfather used to work for Wrigley, a company famous for making chewing gum, as a chemical engineer on a number of different flavor teams. In 2008, Mars, a candy and confectionery company (most famous for M&M's), bought and merged with Wrigley. This is a form of diversification against any one product failing. If something went wrong with gum, the company still has chocolate. If something goes wrong with chocolate, they still have gum.

Your investment portfolio should take a similar approach when it comes to diversifying. Your investment in stocks will take advantage of their potential for long-term gains, while your bonds protect you from incredible market downturns. Similarly, diversification of the types of stocks you own will shield you from financial catastrophe hitting any individual sector.

The problem with this method, however, is that diversification is expensive. One share of Apple (AAPL) is over $180 as of this writing. Simply buying ONE share will cost a lot of money. How could you possibly afford to buy MULTIPLE shares while also buying shares of hundreds, if not thousands, of different companies? It is near impossible. But that's where two important tools come into play: mutual funds and Exchange-Traded Funds (ETFs).

Mutual Funds vs ETFs

A **Mutual Fund** is formed when multiple investors come together and pool their money to provide it to another investor, who invests this money across multiple securities. The investor will then manage the fund, buying and trading stocks and/or bonds based on the particular goals of the fund as well as current market conditions. Using this, a relatively small investment can give you an intense amount of diversification!

While this is a game-changer for easy investing, there are a few drawbacks when it comes to mutual funds. One of the first ones is that there is often a required minimum investment, which can put many small-time or initial investors out of the picture. Second, mutual funds can rack up lots of hidden fees, which can cap their overall return. There are fees that go towards paying the fund manager, marketing the fund, any accounting or legal advice, and so on.

Finally, remember what we mentioned in the section titled Beat the Market. A large majority of actively managed mutual funds don't actually beat the S&P 500, despite all of the resources at their disposal. When they do beat the market, most aren't able to sustain their positive results. When you pay high fees for what is often sub-par performance, you are at risk of severely limiting your growth potential.

Don't get me wrong: mutual funds are often a very important part of a smart investor's portfolio. Be wary of how the fund is set up, and ensure that you aren't completely blunting your returns with high expense ratios. Just a 1% fee can drop your total return by over 17% over 20 years, and when you are dealing with large amounts of money in a retirement account, it amounts to hundreds of thousands of dollars.

The way to combat the fees of actively managed mutual funds is **through Exchange-Traded Funds**, or ETFs for short. First developed in 1993, this was something very similar to a mutual fund: a collection of investors pooled their money in this fund, which aimed to follow or track a particular index or sector of the economy. ETFs are generally very passive, meaning there is much less administrative work that goes into them. Therefore, the cost to you (called the expense ratio) is very low, often well below 0.1%. They also allow for intense diversification, containing hundreds, if not thousands, of stocks and/or bonds. Finally, you can follow individual sectors as well, such as the S&P 500 or small-cap stocks.

When it comes to investing in the stock market, I suggest investing in ETFs that model either the S&P 500 or the total stock market. As I said in the Be the Market section of this chapter, you don't have to fight to exceed the average returns of the market. These funds that mirror the S&P 500 will average 7% and 11% returns and give you the best opportunity to have good, consistent returns over time. You will have ups and downs, but you don't have to worry about finding the next Microsoft, Amazon, or Tesla in order to have a well-performing investment portfolio. Buying the S&P 500 will almost guarantee that you own all of these high-end performers. You don't have to look for the needle in the haystack. Instead, just buy the haystack.

Asset Allocation

Your proportion of your investment portfolio that consists of stocks vs. bonds, or your **asset allocation**, should change as you age. When you are young, you are able to better withstand the drastic market fluctuations that can happen; therefore, you will want to invest *more* in the stock market at a young age. Don't believe me? The market has suffered two major crashes since 2000: The Great Recession of 2008 and the COVID pandemic of 2020. If I had invested $100 in 2007 in the S&P 500, it would be worth $430.12 in 2023, for a total return of over 300% (or 9% per year)! Despite the major financial catastrophes that happened in a 16-year period, keeping money invested yielded highly positive returns.

S&P 500 from 1/1/2007 to 10/19/2023

Data provided by www.macrotrends.net[9]

As you get older, your risk tolerance decreases. You are not able to handle fluctuating prices and potential market crashes at age 65 like you could when you were 35. A stock market crash at age 60 may decimate a portfolio that is heavy in stocks without giving it time to recover before retirement. Therefore, later in life, your asset allocation should consist of more bonds. These will still grow and will protect you from losing a significant portion of your portfolio before retirement. One such sample allocation breakdown is shown below:

Asset Allocation By Age		
Age	Stocks	Bond
30 or Younger	100%	0%
35-40	70%	30%
40-45	65%	35%
45-50	60%	40%
50-55	55%	45%
55-60	50%	50%
60-65	45%	55%
65-70	40%	60%
70-75	35%	65%
75 and Older	30%	70%

Information provided by Financial Samurai[11]

The beauty of this is that it makes investing simple; you don't need to worry about "timing" the market. As shown in the S&P 500 graph above, simply holding your money in the stock market is a surefire way to generate returns. You don't need to worry about which company is better, when to buy or sell, or how to analyze investments. Simply keep a well-diversified portfolio and you'll do just fine.

Investment Accounts

Determining what accounts you use to invest your money is almost as important as the investments that you make. Not each account is built equally, so I'll provide an overview of each of them, as well as why you may wish to use them.

A **brokerage account** can be thought of as your classic, go-to investing account. You put your personal funds into it, invest, and then you can pull that money out when you're ready. When you do, you will need to consider any **capital gains**, or the profit made from the sale of assets, and any possible tax consequences for them. For example, if you buy something for $100 and sell it for $150, the $50 profit (aka capital gain) will be taxed. Tax rates differ depending on the type of capital gain. A **short-term capital gain** is assessed when you hold the asset for less than 1 year and will be taxed at your ordinary tax rate (think the same tax rate as your wages). A **long-term capital gain** is assessed when you hold the asset for longer than one year. These offer a more favorable tax rate than short-term capital gains and can be 0%, 15%, or 20%, depending on the tax bracket you fall into. There are also taxes levied on certain types of monetary distributions, such as dividends. While brokerage accounts don't provide any protection from these taxes, there are other ways that you can invest that will allow you to keep more of the money you earn.

A **401k** or a **403b** are some of the most commonly used retirement accounts and are usually sponsored by employers. You and your employer agree on some amount to put in, up to a maximum legal limit (in 2023, that limit is $22,500). This money gets taken out of your paycheck *before* any taxes are assessed. At that point, it is allowed to grow in the account. When you make withdrawals from the account, taxes are assessed as if they were standard income. There are also no capital gains taxes assessed against these accounts. These are **Tax-Protected** accounts in that the money is not initially taxed when it is put in, and only taxed when money is taken out. It is especially helpful if you are a high earner during your career, as it can help lower your effective tax rate when it comes time to withdraw that money.

Another major benefit to these accounts is that employers often incentivize you to invest in them by having an "employer match." If an employer offers a 5% match, this means they will also make a contribution, dollar-for-dollar, until you contribute up to 5% of the yearly limit. Also of note, this additional contribution does NOT count against your maximum yearly contribution. This is FREE MONEY that the company is offering you! Another way to look at this is that each dollar you put in (up to a limit) will generate one dollar, giving you a 100% rate of return! Not taking advantage of this is insanity.

Generally, you can't withdraw money from a 401k or 403b fund until age 59½ without having to pay taxes on them, along with steep early withdrawal penalties. Therefore, it's best to let that money grow until you reach the proper age. Once you hit a particular age (73–75 in 2023), there are required minimum distributions. These are amounts you are *required* to withdraw from your 401k, whether you need the money or not. This money has grown tax-free for a long time, and the government wants its piece of the pie too!

Next up is a **Roth IRA**. These accounts are a level-up from a 401k. These are accounts where you put in post-tax dollars, and they are allowed to grow. This money is free from taxes as it grows AND when you withdraw it. Because you paid taxes on the money when you put it into the account, taxes are never assessed against it again! This tax-free growth is a major tool that can truly accelerate the growth of your investments more than any other account. There are some stipulations to this as well, which limit your ability to take advantage of it.

First off, there is a limit to how much money you can contribute to the Roth IRA each year. As of 2023, that limit is $6,500 (or $7,500 if you're over 50). Also, there is an income limit, meaning if you make more money than that limit, you are not allowed to contribute money to a Roth IRA. This number is $138,000 for a single individual or $218,000 for a married individual filing jointly in 2023 (if you file separately, you cannot contribute). The way around this second issue is something called a "backdoor Roth IRA." There are many steps that must be followed *to the tee*, but the basics are that you open an individual 401k, contribute $6,500, and have it converted to a Roth IRA. The steps for how to do this can be found with a quick

Google search.

Similar to the 401k, the money in the Roth IRA cannot be accessed until age 59½ without facing a hefty penalty in most circumstances. Simply let the money sit and grow so you can reap the benefits later in life.

The final investment account I want to go over is "non-traditional" for investment purposes, but one that can provide arguably the greatest investment benefits. This is a **Health Savings Account (HSA)**. In a high-deductible health insurance plan, this account allows you to put in your pre-tax dollars and spend them without having to pay taxes, as long as that money goes towards qualified healthcare expenses. What many people don't know is that you can actually *invest* this money in a lot of different funds, depending on which specific group holds the account. This means it has what is called a *triple-tax advantage*: the money is put in tax-free, it grows tax-free, and it can be withdrawn tax-free. It is especially useful as medical care will become more frequent and expensive later in life. You can allow this money to grow and not have to worry about paying for healthcare in your golden years.

Like the other accounts, there are limitations to how your HSA account works. You can spend money from it at any time, but any non-healthcare expenses are subject to taxes and a penalty. Once you turn 65, this penalty goes away, and any non-healthcare withdrawals are taxed as if they were normal income. Finally, there are contribution limits to these accounts as well. In 2023, those limits will be $3,850 for single individuals and $7,750 for families. Even so, it is arguably one of the most powerful savings tools you can have once you max out your Roth IRA and 401k/403b.

Conclusion

This chapter is the most dense and complicated in this book, but arguably the most important in changing your financial life. The steps to financial wellness detail how to invest, so let's pull everything together by revisiting your investments and retirement contributions:

- Save 15–25% of your income for retirement. Use these funds to buy ETFs that mirror the general stock market, as well as bonds or bond funds.
- Your asset allocation should change with your age. Use your young age to your advantage and invest in stock funds, and make your portfolio more heavily invested in bonds as you age.
- Invest first in your company's 401k or 403b to get your employer to match. Then get your Roth IRA maxed out. You can then max out your 401k or 403b. If you still have money to invest to get to your 15%–25% in retirement contributions, use an HSA and taxable brokerage account.

CHAPTER 8: LIFE BEYOND THE BASICS

I wanted to write this book to be filled with quick lessons and to help you start your financial journey. This is not meant to be the end of your financial journey, but rather a jumping-board to more financial education. The basics should allow you to have a comfortable life, but my challenge to you and other readers is to move *beyond* the basics. Maintain your good spending and investing habits while also looking for other opportunities. There are MANY personal finance topics that I haven't covered in this book, which include (but are not limited to):

- Real Estate Investing
- Stock Options
- Penalty-free Retirement Account Withdrawal
- Spending Money in Retirement
- Dollar-cost Averaging vs. Lump Sum Investing

- Cryptocurrency and other Alternative Investments
- When to buy Insurance, and what types of Insurance to buy
- Asset Protection
- Portfolio Rebalancing
- Growth vs. Value Stocks, Small Cap vs. Large Cap Stocks
- Contract Negotiation

And so on. I hope that you explore a lot of these topics on your own. Listen to different voices in the financial community and learn to discern good vs. bad advice, risky vs. conservative advice, and what advice will fit in with, or cause you to change, your financial plan. I'll include some of the resources I use in the appendix. My final goals for you are as follows:

- Find a way to pay off your debt and stay out of it.
- Boring investing is smart investing.
- If people tell you about a "hot stock tip" or try to sell you things, turn around and walk away! Don't deviate from your plan.
- Read at least 2 personal finance books per year, or listen to at least 2 personal finance podcasts or blogs per year. I have included my suggested reading in the appendix of this book.
- ALWAYS keep your vision of a good financial life, and go out and achieve it!

APPENDIX

Sample Excel Budget and Budget Proportion Calculator

The resources in this book are available at my website:

akures1.wixstudio.io/
pocketprosperity

Suggested Reading

- The Total Money Makeover, by Dave Ramsey[12]
  - A long-time financial guru in the personal finance space. His advice is more on the "conservative" side but can be applied to any financial situation in order to get out of debt and build wealth.
  - He also has a company that helps him publish books, develop finance apps, and posts multiple regular podcasts. Find him on YouTube, Spotify, Amazon Music, or your preferred listening platform.

- The White Coat Investor, by Dr Jim Dahle[13]
  - This organization was founded by Dr Dahle, an emergency medicine physician who was tired of the poor financial advice that was given to him and other high-income earners. He has multiple books, a blog, a podcast, multiple courses, and a regular "WCI-Con" which can be used for CME credits
  - As a physician I fit right into his target audience. However, he has

also had blog posts and podcasts dedicated to other professions, such as electrical engineers. Much of his advice is applicable for any profession, but especially those that allow you to earn a high income

- I Will Teach You to be Rich, by Ramit Sethi[14]
  - This book has gone through multiple updates and editions, but is inspiring. This was the first finance-related book that really emphasized *spending* money and building your "rich life." Many people run into a problem where they get to retirement and don't want to spend any money. Ramit urges readers to have a rich-life vision for both today and the future, and his book details how to get there
  - He also has a Netflix show called "How to be Rich," and a podcast where he discusses financial issues with couples. There are always lessons I get from these in terms of the psychology of money

- The Millionaire Next Door, by Thomas J Stanley[15]
  - This is one of the most classic "studies" of millionaires, and how people got to their millionaire status. Although the research is outdated and times have

changed since the first edition of this book, the lesson remains unchanged: Those who live extravagantly often do so at the expense of any savings, while those who save have much to show for it. The typical view of a "millionaire" is generally not what you think it is: the people with large homes, fancy cars, and that go on extravagant vacations often *spend* a million dollars, they don't *have* a million dollars

- The Little Book of Common-Sense Investing, by John Bogle[16]
  - This book is written by one of the founders of the popular investment group Vanguard, and the person who made investing in index funds very popular. In this book he dives into more specifics on the investment strategy I outlined above, and helps you understand the stock market and index funds much better than I ever could

- The Money Guy Show, by Brian Preston and Bo Hanson[17]
  - This is a show I recently stumbled upon. It's a show hosted by Bo and Brian, where they do lots of fun things regarding financial wellness: they take caller questions, they react to bad financial advice on tiktok, and provide

many money lessons
- They also have a website with many free financial resources. These are incredibly useful when trying to organize your thoughts, or have helpful visuals on the effects of saving and investing over time

- The Intelligent Investor, by Benjamin Graham[18]
  - This book is widely regarded as the premier text in the personal investing space. This book is focused on building a portfolio based on the value different companies provide, as opposed to feelings about said companies. It was originally written in 1949, and as a result there are some aspects that may be outdated. However, his advice has continued to ring true for many investors throughout the decades. In fact, Warren Buffet considers it the first book anyone should read before they venture into the space of investing.

WORKS CITED

1. Gailey, A. "Most Americans don't have enough emergency savings, despite the strong labor market." *Bankrate*. 16 Mar 2023, https://www.bankrate.com/personal-finance/emergency-funds-in-strong-job-market/

2. Rubloff, T. "Bankrate's Annual Emergency Fund Report." *Bankrate*. 22 June 2023, https://www.bankrate.com/banking/savings/emergency-savings-report/#key-stats

3. "PolitiFact: 40% of student borrowers lack a four-year degree." *Austin American-Statesman*, 15 September 2022, https://www.statesman.com/story/news/politics/politifact/2022/09/15/fact-check-many-student-loan-borrowers-lack-four-year-college-degree/69493947007/

4. Hanson, M. "Average Student Loan Debt [2023]: by Year, Age & More." *Education Data Initiative*, 22 May

2023, https://educationdata.org/average-student-loan-debt

5. Hannon, K. "Future retirees plan to work longer, partly due to savings shortfalls." *Yahoo Finance*, 15 July 2023, https://finance.yahoo.com/news/future-retirees-plan-to-work-longer-partly-due-to-savings-shortfalls-160038419.html

6. Costa, M. "What's the Average Retirement Savings By Age? - Synchrony Bank." *Synchrony Bank*, 8 9 2023, https://www.synchronybank.com/blog/median-retirement-savings-by-age/

7. May, D. "The 20/3/8 Car-Buying Rule." *The Money Guy Show*, 4 May 2023, https://moneyguy.com/2023/05/20-3-8-rule/"SPIVA | S&P Dow Jones Indices." *S&P Global*, https://www.spglobal.com/spdji/en/research-insights/spiva/

8. Berger, Rob. "4% Rule Definition – Forbes Advisor." *Forbes*, 19 February 2023, https://www.forbes.com/advisor/retirement/four-percent-rule-retirement/. Accessed 20 October 2023.

9. Sommer, J. "Actively Managed Mutual Funds Consistently Fail to Beat Markets, Study Finds." *The New York Times*, 2 December 2022,

https://www.nytimes.com/2022/12/02/business/stock-market-index-funds.html

10. "SPDR S&P 500 ETF - 30 Year Stock Price History | SPY." *Macrotrends*, https://www.macrotrends.net/stocks/charts/SPY/spdr-s-p-500-etf/stock-price-history

11. Financial Samurai. "The Proper Asset Allocation Of Stocks And Bonds By Age." *Financial Samurai*, 23 August 2023, https://www.financialsamurai.com/the-proper-asset-allocation-of-stocks-and-bonds-by-age/

12. Ramsey, D. *The Total Money Makeover: Classic Edition: A Proven Plan for Financial Fitness*. Thomas Nelson, 2013.

13. Dahle, J. *The White Coat Investor's Guide for Students: How Medical and Dental Students Can Secure Their Financial Future*. White Coat Investor, LLC, 2021.

14. Sethi, R. *I Will Teach You To Be Rich*. Workman Publishing Company, 2009.

15. Stanley, T, and William D. Danko. *The Millionaire Next Door: The Surprising Secrets of America's Wealthy*. Taylor Trade Publishing, 1996.

16. Bogle, J. *Little Book of Common Sense*

Investing: The Only Way to Guarantee Your Fair Share of Stock Market Returns. Wiley, 2007.

17. "Blog." *The Money Guy Show*, https://moneyguy.com/blog/. Accessed 20 October 2023.

18. Graham, B, and Zweig, J. *The Intelligent Investor*. Edited by Jason Zweig, HarperCollins, 2006. Accessed 20 October 2023.

ABOUT THE AUTHOR

Alexander Kures

Alex is a medical student who is currently living in the Midwestern United States. He is originally from the Seatlle area, and graduated from Gonzaga University. When he is not learning about personal finance or learning how to save lives,  he enjoys spending time with his wife and his dog.

Learn more at our website!
https://akures1.wixstudio.io/pocketprosperity